Psychedelic Pens
&
A Hopeless
Romantic

Jonathan Miles Berkland

authorHOUSE®

AuthorHouse™
1663 Liberty Drive
Bloomington, IN 47403
www.authorhouse.com
Phone: 1-800-839-8640

First published by AuthorHouse   06/07/2011

ISBN: 978-1-4567-3754-2 (sc)
ISBN: 978-1-4567-3753-5 (ebk)

Library of Congress Control Number: 2011901559

Printed in the United States of America

Any people depicted in stock imagery provided by Thinkstock are models, and such images are being used for illustrative purposes only.
Certain stock imagery © Thinkstock.

This book is printed on acid-free paper.

This book is dedicated to Taylor Swift and love at first performance

FOREWARD

I FEEL I HAVE THE RESPONSIBILITY TO TELL YOU, THE READER (THE BOOK TITLE BEING WHAT IT IS) THAT THIS IS *NOT* A BOOK TRYING TO LEAD YOU TOWARDS A LIFE OF HEAVY DRUG USE. IT IS A BOOK THAT I HOPE WILL HELP YOU ENJOY THE GIFT OF ARTISTICS WITHOUT FEELING YOU HAVE TO CONJOIN THAT WITH DRUG HABITS THAT WILL INHIBIT YOUR SPLENDOR.

EAT A BASIC VITAMIN, EXERCISE, LEND A HELPING HAND, START UP A CHARITY — OR SUPPORT THE CHARITY IDEAS FOUND WITHIN THE TEXTS OF THE MANUSCRIPT, BE ECO-AWARE AND ECO-FRIENDLY, FIND WAYS TO KEEP THE PLANET CLEAN AND HEALTHY, EAT A HEALTHY DIET (PROUD VEGETARIAN), READ UP ON SCIENCE, WRITE A CHILDREN'S BOOK, WORK ON A TV SERIES, BECOME A NOVELIST. THERE ARE SO MANY THINGS OUT THERE TO PRACTICE AND ENJOY WHILE STAYING HEALTHY AND LOVING OTHERS WITHOUT BECOMING OVERLY DRUG OBSESSED. IF YOU TURN TO A LIFE OF DRUGS, I'M NOT ALLOWING YOU TO COME TO ME 10 YEARS DOWN THE ROAD AND SAY, "PSYCHEDELIC PENS & A HOPELESS ROMANTIC MADE ME DO IT."

I'VE SPENT AN <u>UNIMAGINABLE</u> AMOUNT OF TIME ON THIS FIRST BOOK, AND HOPE IT FINDS ITSELF THE RIGHT FANBASE, AND DEEMS ITSELF WORTHY, TO THE READER'S NEEDS. HAVE YOUR PASTELS AND ACRYLIC PAINTS HANDY, THERE ARE PLENTY OF "TURN ME INTO A COLORING BOOK, PRETTY PLEASE" TYPES OF PAGES. FILL IN THE BLANKS WITH SOME TRIPPY PSYCHEDELIC ARTWORK!

I DEDICATED THIS BOOK TO TAYLOR SWIFT PARTLY BECAUSE SHE MADE ME FEEL A TRUE LOVE ALMOST INSTANTLY, AND PARTLY AS A CHALLENGE TO SEE IF I CAN GET ONE OF MY FAVORITE CELEBRITIES TO READ SOME OF MY POETRY AND ARTWORK. SHE'S DEDICATED SO MANY SONGS TO SO MANY GUYS, I FIGURED IT WAS TIME SOMEBODY STEPPED UP AND OFFERED HER SOME LOVE SONGS AND SOME POETRY. IF YOU READ DEEP ENOUGH, LISTEN LONG ENOUGH, WITHIN THE PAUSES YOU MAY FEEL THE PRESENCE OF GREATS.

LONG LIVE EARTH
(AND HOPEFULLY SPACE-TRAVEL)
JMB 2011

Photography is Art
Beauty is Art
Drawings are Art
Paintings are Art
Comedy is Art
Music is Art
Rock & Roll is *damn good* Art
And We are the Artists

TAMA *Volcanic Cactus Photography*

Freedom in the statement
Freedom of a kiss
Freedom of stage presence
Ancient Hieroglyphs

Freedom Freedom Freedom
Freedom says I'm tardy
Get the people amped up
Freedom come and start me

Freedom Writer Say

"Free Neo"

This notebook
Is like
From 1982
Got that artistic vibe too
Is it artistic vibe me?
Or artistic vibe you?
Go to paris?
She's my hue
Fucking cute?
Fucking cute.
Pretty me?
Pretty you.
Club @ 2
Rendezvous
What colors that soul?
Every hue.
Psychedelia
Psychedeli-uh
Psychedeli-a

Me, Dave Grohl, and Taylor Swift were walking through the peach orchard
The golden balloons appeared first, followed by the large, purple caterpillars
with black faces.
A long, bended and curved row of sticks mimicking piano keys appeared.
They funnelled and spiraled upward, then out. Taylor kept whispering to
herself "B minor, B minor, B minor"
We lept – together – and landed on one of the piano keys. A standard G rang
out and echoed and bended back to us. Dave ate a peach and was lifted
upwards. "Up, Up, Up!" Into a rainbow that was painted, arched, and looked
inviting.
A giraffe walked by with a cartoon girl no older than 5 on its back. She took
a black Paul Reed Smith guitar, cried a single tear, and tuned it to a
Dropped D. Dave played a power chord and the bended stairway of piano
keys elevated and we all levitated into a cathedral. "MC Escher is in the
basement drawing". We turned around and two nuns began swaying, like
trees, as their hair became unwound. They brought us to a basin of some
kind of an orangish drink. Both nuns dipped their faces into it. "Would you
like to see where the drink comes from?" I poured some of the orange drink
onto my shoes. They started talking to me.
"We're in Who Framed Roger Rabbit, aren't we?" I looked over to the left
corner of the cathedral. MC Escher was painting a portrait of Taylor sucking
on a candy cane. Dave made a remark I dare not say a second time. It would
offend. I challenged Dave to a man-tall candy cane duel. Taylor was the ref.
"If I win, I'm getting a kiss" I thought to myself.
I told them I'm not leaving until I see a yellow submarine.
They handed me a tangerine. "Damn they're high!" my shoes yelled.
"Is there an italics button in this place, Escher?"
He spoke
"Just wait on the yellow submarine"
"Just wait on the yellow submarine"
"Just wait on the yellow submarine"

Tell us another tale, they said
So that's what I'm here to do
I don't like what has been done to terrify you
But I sure would like to entertain you

Instead of a violent image
Why don't we write the world another song
Or even better yet
Stop the violence all-together, sound another world gong

Keep the peace strong
This is Bonjour
Yeah hit the peace gong
Jamaica rips that peace bong
People stand strong
"I come from the streets, Boi!"
And all we wanna do is watch her play with that new sex t-oi!"

"Now kids bring your rubbers,
I know you love rapping inside hummers
But the girls beyond those doors
Are some real fucking stunners
And they want you all under the covers
So can you please just be some good boys?"

"Yes mom, but can I still bring some sex toys?"

"You kids are dogs, but this is getting out of my control. Fuck tards, I'm
going looney, maybe I could use some of those exotic bowls"

"Bout time!"

Keep the peace strong
There is no such thing as Au Revoir
Because the world
Has got time left
And when it doesn't
We'll save
This earth
Into jars

The self In Two Prisms
Aligned By Nine Herbs
The Tangents Keep Growing
Welcome To My Third
Dementia's Dimensions
Are Porcelain Dolls
The Blue-Bellied Children
Inch Their Way Through Our Halls
Now A Light Show Of Faces In Purple And Red
They Mask Gods In Rhythm As They Dance Through Our Head
And These Blue-Bellied Children Grasp Ahold Their own Bolt
And Paint Arcs Of Lightning As Time Rows Their Boat

Hero
Interfusion
Soil
Empire of the sun
Outskirts
Fragments
Forces
Tao
Odyssey

The canoes no longer in use
Now lizards crawl inside.
The pumpkin patch and pirate's batch
The orchard's punch
And trailing scent of merchant spices
And fairy nectars
The love making on the beach
The money bags filled with candle wax,
Black resins, and cypress oils.
The carefully woven pipes and ancient looking oil lamps.
Smoking lamps and lightbulbs, dancing...
In the flames.
Right in front of the totem poles
The black sand & scattered turquoise stone
The rainbow-colored birds and pirate's musket
The smell of the cornish hens, potatoes, and soups
So pleasurable you'd have walked the beach, collecting the turquoise Stones
with one of the concubines for a heapful.
A kiss from the concubine & shared laughter on these black sands.
The electricity of the night set in and a large group of those on shore
Jumped in the water, just underneath the Aurora Borealis
The laughter and frolics made all feel welcome
And most felt a sweet divine set in
The drifting smell of the salted hens and soups lingered to them,
Solidifying the fact that within the hour a feast was to be had.
They took a mild sedative and watched the lizards run along, atop the water.
Then untied one of the giant,
Wooden boats and let it start to drift out to sea.
They would wait an hour, until the boat had fallen back
A few hundred feet back into the ocean
And then swim to it.
But first they must fill it with goodies and surprises
So that when they finally swam out and got on the boat,
Naked and alive,
They would feast in an orgy of laughter under the moonlight.
Candles, candies, mirrors, magic-looking stones...
All were placed in the cabins and private quarters.
Everyone laughed
Watched the boat drift
And massaged each other's backs
With hot oil on the black sands

Show me how to love myself
And I'll show you a true smile
Tell me all the things you love
And I'll stay here for a while
Don't know where to go from here
Most likely it's alone
The only things it feels I have
A master and a home
But then my brother calls to me
"Why must you look so down?"
Rebellion from hypocrisy
That's why I wear this frown

Together I know we can make things right
Our heroes sacrificing through the night
So here we pray that through faith we'll shed light
Two lonesomes, Two lonesomes, Two lonesomes

I Want To Pray
With The Forces of The Wind and The Rain

All I'm trying to do
Is write another love song
Wondering if theres any other woman out there who cares
Other than
My mom

What am I supposed to do
When I want to write a sex song!

Only a few truly know
About my ultimate suffering
Maybe the prayers I made to God
To end up a victory story
Are gonna pay off

All I'm trying to do
Is write another love song
Romantic Freedom Writer wants to be heard
Is that so wrong?

My pastor told me from here on out
Hes going to read every one of my songs

Now what am I supposed to do
When I want to write a sex song?

Think of each day as a challenge
That takes a definite balance
Of letting go, striving onwards, and earning an allowance
Moving on past the talus

We learn the process of climbing
Subjectively magnifying
Steadily multiplying

Reach the top tier
And baby girl we're flying

Weird
Propaganda
Its weird propaganda
Selling
Themselves
They're selling themselves
Open
Suggestions
Heard open suggestions
Thinking
Outside
I'm thinking outside

Blatant
Malfunctions
His blatant malfunctions
Heartful
Distress
Her heartful distress
Imperfect
Together
They're imperfect together
Weird
Propaganda
Its weird propaganda

Do you feel the shaking girl, all alone on city streets
Do you wish you had a blanket to wrap around her as she sleeps
Give her housing, loving comfort, new strength, warm blankets, something
To eat
Sometimes I ask myself why there seem to be so few avenues to truly help

Phoenomenons are discovered
Sometimes stumbled upon

Like a true love
Being found
And held dear

I want to show the world
True love
For glory comes
When
True love is felt

Wherever she may lay
That precious love of mine
Tell her I love her already
And I'm sorry it's taking so long
Yes, I'm sorry I'm taking so long
But I'll more than make it up when I find you

During the war
I dream of Keira
Theres no need to dream of genie

I can dream her up
There are purple flowers in her hair
Rain water and flower nectars dripping off of her face
Dreaming of love and laughs where we can become nudists and
Run through space
Where I can put on a head-dress and act like a pirate
All she'll needs now
Is such a beautiful compilation
Where's Taylor's guitar?
I could weep at her feet

Prayers for safety and refuge
And America's freedom bells found in words

Let love conquer all
For there comes laughter
And ever afters
Sealed, with love
My gift to you

If they were to make a movie of your life
It's a given the main character dies
But what's unexplainable
Is how his soul is born again
And this time
He flies

Oh, how apparent that you're here for a real reason
I pray to God the father that you never stop believing

Writing in the dark
Playing in the park
Always feels theres something missing
On this trip which we've embarked
One is all alone
The others leaving home
Going out or looking in, there's endless space to roam
He puts down his camera
She puts on her coat
This picturesque mantle just became the centerpiece

Escaping from his coldness
Stepping to the winter night
Keeping warm by the fire, she knows why he takes flight
Everybody listens
When they're told they'll glisten

Now shine, beloved stars
Now shine, shine, shine
Shine on your crazy diamonds
Just shine! Shine! Shine!
One day I'll have a sweetheart
And make you mine, mine, mine

The love artist
Brought us
A piece of destiny
The poet princess in the castle
Called down from the balcony

Romeo
Loverboy
Drummer Boy
Socrates

Sunflowers in June
Love Potions for July
Dreamers
Who know exactly why we cry
Suffered Hard
So I'm Alive like a Cherry Bomb

Loner Romeo
Angels & Airwaves
Can you send some love to my
Favorite Blonde
Cherry Bomb

All my efforts
Are etched into tomes
All my misery
Turned to slow rock suicide

The poet princess
Might feel the beating of this heart
While its alive

Pat on the back for keeping Marley's legend alive
We catch a fire then we catch a vibe
The smokey forefront made to hypnotize
Undid discrepancies to keep it live

My dream girl
Plays acoustic guitar
Our speaker systems
Bump
Hard
Shake the ground

Our speaker systems
Bump
Hard
Shake the ground

Pat on the back for keeping Marley's legend alive
We catch a fire then we catch a vibe
The smokey forefront made to hypnotize
Undid discrepancies to keep it live

There's a natural mystic blowin through the air

Of mice and men
The thought, through pen
Must branch and reach to touch again
Birthed questions with each morning's -
Dew the dying yearn to breathe again
Or is their last our breeze 'pon shore

It's become apparent
Paper can't hold my deepest thoughts
They unravel, winged and without words
Dreams, humbling needs,
A star is walking towards a yacht
Constructing archways, golden
Did Dali need to cue the hue
Or was it light within his limbs
Fueling to spark each and every clue
All of us invite you to
The voices of the romantics

I've become a critic
Of walking upon shore
The waves are so enticing
Deep echoes forevermore

Her soothing touch aquatic
And so I dive on in
A mix of lust with nature's touch
We swam away from sin

When we reached our safe haven
Walking tranquility's path
Her touch, her stare, her essence, air
Her bubble made my bath

For once it felt so lonely
My walk on London Bridge
No longer does it wish to fall
I'd rather taste her ridge

Excuse me miss, you've lost your marbles
Would you like to share mine?

Yes, your road has spoken to me
Sounding frantic, empty highway
So full of life
Full of care
With each echo she makes
My spirit's awe becomes – a stare
I'll paint the world upon your lips
Ease the pain between your hips
Resonate your need to feel
What is true
What is real
This moment wasn't meant for me
Behind the scenes, watching you truly see
Our waves break, roaring like the crowd
Watching, waiting, listening...no sound

Where have these two lovers gone
Who sang us to tears through moving song
They left abruptly to the clouds
Stroking her cadence
They shan't be found

Woven amongst the reed
Which reads a proclamation's tender tune
Tune your G to A
Your T to E
And harmony is found
In the next room

Alone, Alone
If those who have passed can find
Heaven
Under a moon and a silver light
They would probably teach us
Of kisses

There is an essence beating
Beating odds and bearing life
There is a lifeless knowledge
Bearing fruit to the soil

Charity work
10,000 basins of mint water
Bulk green tea
For the teary-eyed
Sons and daughters
Their tears shed
Are truly holy water
But their basin
Is running dry
Yes their basin
Is running dry

You say all hope of help is gone, but
I know someone who can
World Vision
I challenge thee
10,000 basins of mint water

I dream
As does the artist
Her soul a golden brush
See she and I mutually fly
Soaring, we share a smile's thrust
Realized extensions of our being
Shall pronounce a Holy Ohm
Now these blessed children fingerpaint
My mind, Rosetta Stone
And once decreed, We'll leave at once
To set a distant shore
Known not, a final resting place
Known not, yet out the doors
Of truth, of light
Of conscious flight
Endured to know Thy Lord
And so I sit here weeping
The artist by my side
We're shown the blooming flower
When will our soul be free to glide

Where are the just who will lead
They who shall succeed
Don't want my children to believe
The loss of a life is worth oil and greed
When they look to the sky
Somewhat like chasing a high
Will they wonder with astonishment
That which enable us to fly
One thing I'll tell them is this
A perfect key, A perfect wish
The Creator allows creation through our dream's loving kiss

So smolder me with questions
The answers seem to speak themselves
Fate handed you its magnitude
And smiled back to new-found wealth
Did the piper play for you a love song?
Was he at the gates of dawn?
Did he awaken you with fragrant tunes
Which moistened sorrow with "so long"
If so, you fly alongside
All the triumphs of today
Then look upon the eagle
Making haste, and making way

My brother says he's from neptune
So I pick up my earth sticks
Rhythmatically, I speak neptunian sounds

Get free
They're high like hippies

The revolution & the future of rock & roll are in love with me
Yeah
I'm in love with them
Yeah
The revolution & the future of rock & roll
Are all that's left worth clinging on to
Yeah
I'm in love with them
Yeah
I'm in love with them

We're rocking again
I'm fluid with a pen
If they want to see the epitome of a guitar player
I'm bringing little brother in

Message in a bottle
If messages can carry on

"I get psychedelic with a pen and a pad"

Listen to Au Revoir Simone

Night Fashioned in Luminescence
A tranquil path of stardust to the moon
Each glow, down to her faintest, fragranced the mind with Vision
And the soul with a reassuring embrace
As we rowed our way through
Holiest of Realms

What we do with this gift we're given
Is a testament to the living
As is a sentiment for those who've passed
Told from a regiment
Timeless past

Root Beer
& Melatonin

Drink Makers
& Dream Makers
& Bud Makers
& Spud Makers
& Love makers

Just to be an artist
One both thrives & suffers through
Aspirations of conjuring up and believing in
A realm so unlike the one we're living in
The orphanage has its pixie dust on hold

Philosopher. Alien. Dreamer.
Poet. Sculptor. Muse.
Did Jasmine plant salvation too?
Next to the lilly-pad laced lullabys
A golden marinade warms sinew

Don't ask the weavers what they're weaving
Or the elves of their construct

The Ancient Monks are artists
Working on orbs & spheres
With magic in every hue

Find the common denominator
Of what makes you better
What makes you faster
What makes you stronger
Where your talents flourish
When your successes boom
Find entertainment & love
Happiness & peace
Be Jason, discontent until he masters the fleece

Lord just come to me
And tell me how to save their souls
No more oppression, broken-heartedness, or empty bowls

Freedom Writers
Fuck shackles!
Do a rain dance!
Get that soul back
Make it groovy
Let that soul trance
Let that girl dance
I'll take her to the ball
And if you've got a drumkit nearby
We'll cover Wonder Wall

Leave the spirits all in awe
Like a cascading waterfall
Our song is meditation mixed with genius
Mixed with freedom mixed with awe

Soul
Mate

All alone writing
Love stories for barren hearts

We're in the Clouds Of Smoke
A Purple Dust
In The Breeze

Swimming through the sands of time

The past moves aside
And life comes in

Paiste cymbals
Psilocybin & D.W. McQuarters
D.W. McQuarters & a blonde
I can't seem to remember
Because they were stolen
Return them to me
Like my talents in drawing
Inspired in a
Characteristic top-hat

Sometimes you've just gotta write.....

I hope the love of 60 year olds
Is genuine and true
Mind beaten down
Twenties, but blue
I'm bluer than jazz
It hurts too bad to be a compliment

This hole is beating my mind
Let us find another remedy

Remedy Remedy
Remedy My Soul
Don't keep me around if she's not going to join

It's so sad being alone
Without her cuddles to my throne

It gets me down
So down
So down
When I'm alone

Maine
Guitars
Drifting off to sleep
Wond'ring whats in store
On the other side of eternity
If good friends are involved, my vote is some good, free souls
I mapped them out like a musical path, so smoothly

They say this ones a sweetheart
So I qued my glow, and dusted off my wick
And surprised you in your dreams
My darling, the peppermint stick

Follow the glowing lanterns
Row of lanterns in the trees

Neon, Neon
Neon, Neon

You sit on a frozen throne
Waiting for The One
Living in a defined world
Only to become
The One

Almighty Essence of Divinity
I Ask You To Bless Me On This Day
Composing Symphony Infinity
In The Light-Dispersing Day

My oh my I've caught a buzz!
To infinity and beyond!

The man who has looked within
Is the man who has gained perspective

It should not be such a grueling, painful, heart-wrenching thing
To find Love
Building upon it, however
Will forever remain a work in progress

So alone in bed
Looking to my empty vastness
I continue to faithfully cry
My lifelong ode to you

Freedom Flows
Fluid Pen
Stopping to
Be born again
The question not
Was it then or now
The question brought
Like a floating gown
The seamstress wove
The maiden's fears
The husband gave
Rainforest tears

Energy. Synergy
Synchronized Flow
Ambivalent Intelligence
The Ginkgo Tree's Prose
Elephant Harpsichords
Whispered Lullaby Hymns
Pigmented Wisdom
Wondered Through Elder's Grins
Catch-Phrased Euphoria
Catches the felt of my pen
If One Truly Listens
They'll Listen Again

I'll open up The Space Trails
And begin to search for life
When this body here is laid to rest with earth
The solar system's footsteps,
Oh what Holy Lamps we have
It is these very lamps that lead from war and strife

Bring your camera
Bring your journal
My friend, you're going to have it all
Yes the soul is quite equipped with masquerading wonderballs
And these realms awaiting beckon you to taste their hidden waterfalls
Still unstirred by human hands, blooming strands of wond'rous awe

So enlighten all your senses at The Cooling of Whirl Pool
Entertain the nymphs with cloaking clovers
Their Grandfather-seed stems from The Moon
Thank the force of mount saint mary there's no being home by noon
As mothers whisper softly to their daughter's ear
"He's going to be here soon"

What does it mean
To be a Student of the Lord
How does one break free

Your morals carve a gift of light
A holy crystal satellite

I came to say I love you

I am the Silver Surfer
I am the Iron Lung
I am The Hieroglyphics
I am The Chosen One
I am Fire On Your Tongue
Like A Psychedelic Sun

"Now drum you little fucking alien!"

Light the incense
Cali skateboard
All respects & a gauge
Earings man
Fuck with range
Set a view
And the stage

Snowy peak
These are not lights
They're more like lanterns
They light up
Let us see the pictures on the walls
These hieroglyphics
Of Purple Moose
With Purple Antler
With Purple Crayon
With Purple Candle
We're setting course
For a deep-snow land
Frost on the sword
I'm putting on my armor
Blessed with Runestones
Not tombstones

I like the spherical,
The spherical mass
The spherical mass
That reverberates somethin spiritual

Worldly Knowledge
Respect the Earth
End Pollution
Legalize Freedom

Giving up
I'm giving up
Why did I even begin
I was born to hold drumsticks
Drumsticks, not a pen

Masturbation in public!

The Tibetan Monk is Silent
Tonight

I'm in search of
Sphinxes, Sand Statues
Stone Henge – Stone Rock
If I ever show up
I'm cruisin down the block
With a driver up front
And a hookah in the trunk
And a Crutchfield singin "B-Bump B-Bump Bump"

Music note,
Floating through the sky

❧Soak The Grotto, Ride The Lizard, Fuck The Maid☙
Good king, like the crops from the king's shore
Good king, like the crops from the king's shore

Musical Creativity
Musical Experimentation
Grow Cactus
Bang Beat
Art The Nation

If Asperatus comes
Then Asperatus sounds
And if Asperatus comes
We earn our lovelies gowns

Through Stone Henge Eye
Through Stone Henge Eye
Through Stone Henge Eye

I Like Shoreside Attractions
Who Kiss Your In-between the lines
Mixer, Mixer Ancient Hieroglyphics
Writing To You With Love
Like A Daughter's Favorite Lullaby

❧God Is In The Breeze❧

I pray
That granny is there
To bless
My marriage

Have I escaped the tomb?
Am I within the womb?
To eat and drink of afterlife
Our dreams must search new rooms

The Next Chapter
Always meets "the hereafter" with a grin
While paving the unique destiny
Our desires chase for a closing door
Of course we met "Experience"
More than a friendly passing by
These wings almost draw themselves as we
Discover life without
A second look
And the external art says we must take a third
Yes our God has painted delicacies
Which resonate from outer worlds

It was Immaculate, Immortal
Soul, Spirit, and Portal
What will man trade control for?
A consciously new order
Do we pass through the flames to reach her?
To Love and continue to teach her?
Her beauty's within her creature
She's a human. Special features

Feeling like eternity
Without a queen's throne next to me
A broken hearted king
I've suffered too frequently
Forsaken
Almost etched it in ink
I've lost a piece of my soul
I think
Cuz she's not here
And I'm not alright
I'm alone
Like every single fucking night
My soul
Bleeds without her presence
I believe
A smile is a shared present

Take my work
A turquoise necklace
And spin the spinner's soul

I'm trained
My tears, the music's wetness

The Moon & The Tide
Shall Align With The Vine
Powerful Puff.....
Just Let The Ninja Tune

There Was A Triangle
But He Wouldn't Go Off The Beaten Path
And The Music's Tune Is
A Hierarchy Of
Cobblestone, Black Wood & Stilts
❧& Sunshine☙
All Playing The Part In
One Verse. One Verse.
Uni Verse.
One Verse.

You Fuckin Give Me The Key

Remember When You Handed Me Two Sticks
You Gave Me The Key

The White Owl
Often Stays At Home
No Not His Soul
His Soul Is Free To Roam

Pray For Safety
Pray For Rain
& Pray For Her
In The Fashion You Deem Necessary

And Yes, The Zeppelin's Lead

We Will Taste Like Psychedelic Melons

Jonathan Miles Berkland

Chill Peace Love Fun
So emotion, keep it real
The Sun, The Clouds
The Portrait of Jamaica

An Artist
All vibe!
Stay happy
Stay amused
Stay, Stay for me
Let some souls free, then
Hip hop hip hop hip hop
Don't stop the rock if
John Stocktons in the park
311 Blue Album says
I've earned some kisses in the dark
I hope she's coming to the reflection of the glow sticks
I hope I stumble into my own Penny Lane
I hope that sweet country thing named Taylor takes names
I write passion, the spirit of the flame
311 is just about to take stage

311 *Volcanic Cactus Photography*

❧In the planetarium☙
✦✦✦✦✦✦✦✦✦✦✦✦✦✦
℘The ceiling is covered in stars℃

Drumming in the Observatory
Star Light & Hand Drums
The Dune & The Constellation
The Instruments & The Incense
The Djembe & The Crowd

The Colors
The Lifeforce
The Spectrum
The Groove

The Path of Righteousness
Placed lilacs in your dreams and soothed you with scented oils
It freed your chains
And found your misplaced crown
In the most glorious of chariots
Our souls mouthed their goodbyes
Together imprinting the dust

The rain is pattering on the road
The desert valley crawling with lizards, geckos & wanderers
Blessed by the moon children

The Dry, Red Brick clay
Bowing to the splendor

We fall deep
Into
The Purple Sun's Setting
Like a tablecloth
Pictures of Ancient Aztecs & large cloth napkins of avacadoes
Mysteries of Crystal Skulls being dipped into rainbow-colors

Rainbow Colors

All the reds became greens
All the blacks melt
With purples and magentas
Maybe we learn
To break free of some rules
To break free of some traffics
When we stop being
So cynical
And create
Something more magic

Black Currants
& The funky beat jazz
Miles Davis
Herbie's Herbs
A Pound of Blackberries
& A Smoking Lamp

Drink from the well of the hypnotic sounds
Melodic clouds
From their tranquil grounds
If they're feelin your vibe
Then your stayin the night
& I'm buyin new pillows
To help me dream of you tonight

Symphonies call to me
Like God's ringtone
Our Love
Only seems to glimpse at it's throne
Although theres a chance
It's never seen it before
Don't blame it, my love
It's been on a journey

Teardrops on the lovers
Reflections made of glass

Writers for the centuries
Can exemplify
Freedom with a Pen

I'm searching for some peace of mind
Aromatic strands you've left behind
Where a longing heart intertwines itself admidst the breeze

I'm seeking out the hidden doors
Which take us to such blissful shores
Where we're moved by spirit
And there are no wars extended to our kin
I'm reaching out and stepping in
Abroad spectrums unknown to men
Reminding the self the realm we're in
Is not all we're to know

You have creative control over your soul
Find sources of inspiration
Wells
Pools of water in creviced rocks
Aquaducts
Seek out temples of light

To heal your present, guide your night
Fill glass lightbulbs up with water
Make them a backdrop to the night

Norway shores sound
All too nice

Once upon a story
Yes this is how it goes
It's about old silly willy billy
Who was known for putting on shows
Third-floor windows
No curtains or blinds
First night of the show
He shows his behind
Night two
Move down
He changed to the second floor
Then changed into hair & makeup
And sprawled out drunk on the floor
He had fights with sex toys
And sock monkeys, too
The townspeople love him
What are we to do?

What is the Tao of Now? I see a peaceful revelation
When Sgt. Pepper plays, it revives a dying nation

The teardrops of "I love you"
Replentishing all creatures who care
Like limbs of oak, branching out to taste
Sweetness of the air

A still of utter calmness
Hencing the fiercest storm
Like seedlings of the dandelion
Anticipating to be born

With young ones gliding out the door
Reinforcing "It's Alright"
They'll rise above and grow to be
The ones who conquer night

I hear the pianos in the hallways
Marvelin at murals
From Picaso to Monet
Twisting Lime Drinks in Bombay
I hardly know what to say
All this love I can give

Sobering sidewalks
Clustering sky
Occulant oysters
Prying my eye
What are they seeking
Who do they know
Why do they tell me
"Pee in the snow"
Sounding so honest
Distortion & air
5-toed pigmentations
Disperce from my hair

Senseless as candles
Dumbfounding wicks
Grandmothers, feed me
Cranberry fix

Twenty years
Of building up my defenses
Twenty years
Through blood through tears
Through ice through storm
My fire burns against the norm

A thousand tears
At the so-called mercy of torture, lost love, and solitude
A thousand tears
Awaiting a chance to drench thine own parched lips
Knowing future tales say I must crawl

I rise above
And call unto you
And in these times I am Oasis

There's always a higher calling
I'm searching for mine still
It feels like jumping out of a helicopter
For us, For Love, Free will

You've got to know not to overdose
I've gotta break on through

For you
For you
For you
For you
And you
And you
And you

Be Turbulent Don Paragon
Juan Crespo, Don Juan

Enchanted are the marigolds
Inviting as one

It didn't have a name
The spirit of the flame
It dabbed the artist's brain
Her river wood his rain

A daughter ever born
Would know my Love as I'm reborn
Together seeking out true flight
Forever Students on The Way

Oh the nourishment of the soul
Her origami & I fold
This precious gift begs to be heard
And my heart longs to listen

So step by step I weave dreamcatchers
And pray they find their rightful name
Handcrafted for her fantasies
Like a dandelion's breeze

Make a stand as a musician

❧

Root
Clay
Snow
❧

We are rocks
High and mighty
Take shape

The Tip Top, Lets Make A New Page
Just The Ninth Cloud
Fragrant Ocean & Earth Bound
The Symphonics Of Our Sounds
Telecasters & Hip-Hop Beats & Sounds
Grandfather Clocks
And Turbulent, Turbulent Sounds

The Crow Of The Ring
The Ring Of The Sound

We're Falling Asleep
To Victorious Sounds

Blonde-haired & so alive
A blessing for my dreams
These clouds can get so lonely
❧Orchestra☙
Percussively, the strings
Are singing what it means

Because she is my angel
Because she is my dove
Because I need her in my favorite dreams
Because we're spacebound, to Love

In the body there lies a temple
Strictly elemental

Love
The private parts of your self
They are yours
And yours alone

 Jonathan Miles Berkland

A little rebel music
Was all that we needed
Drive Route 66
Alone while
My pen's bleedin
Open up your mind like a tractor beam
Let the good guys in

If you need an uplifter
We can come
And do this shit again

If you need an uplifter
Just put me on
Again

Mom,
Put down the gin!
Drunker than a mexican!
On the verge of Summer of the Monkeys
Just run around
Make pretend

This rhythms so Three One One
I'll FOABT to bring it in

Soulful like Jazz
Hey-ey e-ey e-ey
It's over too fast
Hey-ey e-ey e-ey
Hope blondie saves me fast
Hey-ey e-ey e-ey
I'll say
I found bouyency at last
Hey-ey e-ey e-ey

The romantics are alive tonight
One of us feels
Slightly saddened,
Slightly tragic
That no lovers lips are upon mine

Hopeful still
Perhaps it is the
Love and the lust
That keeps me going

Through the power of prayer
We will try
And help heal the land

Longing for her embrace
Praying for the safety
And to help heal
Our parties

Blessings
Upon the lands
Like rainforest tears they call

They give life
They give shelter

I bathe in the rain
And love it as it extinguishes flames

The rain & the canopy
The fears I dash away with the power
Of prayer
And of touch

Will she feel it?
Is it holy?

The present
Would love her dearly

True love
Doesn't walk my way too often
It caught my eye in a country world
Blonde hair in a blossom
Some of those girls out there said
"Tease, Tease, Tease me!"
This one took flight
SNL
MTV

Don't sign me on for fortune or fame
I just want you to hear my love
Such a fragile thing
"Dad, don't let them shoot down that dove"
If they do
Theres gonna be a rookie in the Air Force
Freedom Writer
Peace is always what we're aimin for

Don't you remember
Peace of Mind found
Don't you remember
Peace of Mind found

Music is our favorite medicine
So sing it out loud
Sing it out loud
Sing it out loud
Sing it out loud
Sing it out loud

Fireflies in maine
Were all me & mom needed that night

Getting lonely,
She's longing for England again
"Boy how you gonna get me there?"
"Your just a loner with a pen!"

Smiles shared in maine
Catching fireflies
Out in the garden

They say that goodbyes
Always gonna be the hardest

You might've given up on me
But I will not give up on you

Saying hello to England
Is something your gonna do

Smiles shared in maine
Catching fireflies
Out in the garden

Never turn joys to tears
Never turn love to fear

A wild, beating heart
That wants to speak
To speak now

They say "Give it all you've got"
The love artist by my side

Reach for the stars
Was all he could do
Doesn't know much of romance
But said he'd love to do a little more
Than feel abandoned by such joys
This romantic writer
Is writing for you

Said he'd love to look through
And into her heart

He said it looked a little more true
Windows of the soul took me
To a tennessee hue

They say "Give it all you've got"
The love artist by my side
The chances a million to one
Those other hearts were not mine
A million and one more acoustic
Guitars that said "Stand aside, we're movin on through"
Now theres acoustic guitars
Who almost seem to be named after you